RACE
AND
SPORTS

RACE IN SPORTS MEDIA COVERAGE

BY DUCHESS HARRIS, JD, PHD
WITH JILL C. WHEELER

Essential Library

An Imprint of Abdo Publishing | abdobooks.com

ABDOBOOKS.COM

Published by Abdo Publishing, a division of ABDO, PO Box 398166, Minneapolis, Minnesota 55439. Copyright © 2019 by Abdo Consulting Group, Inc. International copyrights reserved in all countries. No part of this book may be reproduced in any form without written permission from the publisher. Essential Library™ is a trademark and logo of Abdo Publishing.

Printed in the United States of America, North Mankato, Minnesota
092018
012019

Cover Photo: Liu Zishan/Shutterstock Images
Interior Photos: Bob Thomas/Popperfoto/Getty Images, 5; Atlanta Journal-Constitution/ AP Images, 7; Bettmann/Getty Images, 12; Matty Zimmerman/AP Images, 15; Buyenlarge/Archive Photos/Getty Images, 17; AP Images, 21, 25, 30, 33, 37, 41, 49, 95; John Cordes/Icon Sportswire/AP Images, 34; Paul Spinelli/AP Images, 46, 47 (top); Cheriss May/NurPhoto/Sipa USA/AP Images, 47 (middle); Al Messerschmidt/AP Images, 47 (bottom), 59; Richard Drew/AP Images, 51; Lennox McLendon/AP Images, 54; Haraz N. Ghanbari/AP Images, 63; Gene J. Puskar/AP Images, 66; Jeff Chiu/AP Images, 71; Anthony Nesmith/Cal Sport Media/AP Images, 75; Robert Beck/Sports Illustrated/Getty Images, 77; Doug Mills/AP Images, 81; Bill Clark/CQ Roll Call/AP Images, 84; Kyle Grillot/Sipa USA/ AP Images, 91

Editor: Patrick Donnelly
Series Designer: Craig Hinton

LIBRARY OF CONGRESS CONTROL NUMBER: 2018947976

PUBLISHER'S CATALOGING-IN-PUBLICATION DATA

Names: Harris, Duchess, author. | Wheeler, Jill C., author.
Title: Race in sports media coverage / by Duchess Harris and Jill C. Wheeler.
Description: Minneapolis, Minnesota : Abdo Publishing, 2019 | Series: Race and sports |
    Includes online resources and index.
Identifiers: ISBN 9781532116742 (lib. bdg.) | ISBN 9781532159589 (ebook)
Subjects: LCSH: Press coverage--Juvenile literature. | Racism in sports--Juvenile
    literature. | Race relations--Juvenile literature. | Sports--Juvenile literature.
Classification: DDC 796.089--dc23

CONTENTS

CHAPTER ONE

JACK JOHNSON VS. JIM CROW

T he event captured the attention of the world. On July 4, 1910, after months of promotion and discussion, heavyweight boxer Jack Johnson stepped into the ring with former world heavyweight champ James Jeffries. It might have been just another fight except for one critical fact: Jeffries was white, and Johnson was black.

The fight was years in the making. John Arthur "Jack" Johnson was born in 1878 in Galveston, Texas, to formerly enslaved people. He was attracted to a life of adventure. As a teen, he stowed away on a ship bound for New York City, eventually making his way to Boston, Massachusetts. That's where he met boxer Joe Walcott and began considering a career in the ring. Returning to Galveston, he began to make his own name as a fighter. By the early 1900s, he was considered a contender for the world heavyweight title. There was just one problem. No black fighter had ever been allowed to compete for that honor.

Johnson was born at the end of Reconstruction, the time that immediately followed the US Civil War (1861–1865). With slavery outlawed, Southern states began to adopt laws to segregate white and black people. These laws and the system they created became known as Jim Crow.

Marchers protest segregation in Atlanta, Georgia, in 1961.

Jim Crow became a barrier for Johnson on multiple fronts. It hampered his ability to be recognized as a champion. It also reduced his ability to earn a living. By 1900, boxing had become more of an entertainment spectacle than a sporting event. The fight itself was just the beginning. Films of fights were popular at local movie theaters and often ended up in screenings around the world. Yet the biggest purses—the prize money the boxers fight for—and most successful films were reserved for contests between two white fighters. Black fighters competed for far smaller payouts. Meanwhile, Jim Crow also meant that black fans had to watch the fight films in black-only theaters, or in the sections of white-run theaters where black customers were allowed to sit. Likewise, fight fans could only read about matches between two black fighters in black newspapers.

"HOPE OF THE WHITE RACE"

Jim Crow or not, Johnson was determined. He took aim at reigning heavyweight champ Tommy Burns. He taunted the white Canadian fighter in the press and followed him from England to Australia. Burns told reporters that he disliked black people, and he especially disliked Johnson.

Johnson finally got his title fight on December 26, 1908. He dominated the contest, with officials stopping it in the fourteenth round for fear of further injury to Burns. Johnson was now officially the world heavyweight champion. He celebrated by jumping up and shadowboxing for the cameras. Referring to Johnson's African roots in a stereotypical fashion, one Australian reporter characterized the victory celebration as "a triumphant war dance—like the dance after the battle, before the cannibal feast began."[1]

Around the world, the victory sparked pride in the black community and concern among white people. Not only had Johnson dared to fight and defeat a white man—he also fought Jim Crow. He refused to act in the way most white people at that time believed black people should act. He dressed in fancy clothes. He drove nice cars. He dated white women. He spoke his mind. Johnson wanted the world to recognize him as the champion.

Yet most white boxing fans at that time refused to accept a black heavyweight champion. They wanted him to lose—especially to a white man. A campaign began in the media to have Johnson fight Jeffries, the former world heavyweight champion. Jeffries had retired from the sport in 1905, and he had refused to face black fighters throughout his career. Yet in the eyes of many, he was the last hope to beat Johnson. Newspapers began referring to the now heavier and out-of-shape Jeffries as the "Hope of the White Race."[2] Jeffries bowed to the pressure and agreed in late 1909 to fight Johnson.

THE ROOTS OF BLACK BOXING

Black boxing in the United States traced its roots to a multi-fighter combat sport called the battle royal. The tradition began in medieval Europe. It made its way to the American colonies, where it became a practice among slaves. At first, slaves engaged in battle royals for their own entertainment. The practice later became a part of Jim Crow discrimination.

In a battle royal, anywhere from four to 30 black men and boys would be blindfolded and set to fighting one another. The fight continued until one lone victor remained standing. Such battle royal events were arranged for the benefit of a typically white audience, and the winner received only a few dollars for his efforts. Newspaper records point to battle royals promoted at carnivals, fairs, and other gatherings around the United States from the late 1800s to as recently as 1950. Both Jack Johnson and lightweight champion Joe Gans triumphed in battle royals early in their careers.

BLATANT RACISM IN MEDIA

The concept of objective news coverage is a recent phenomenon. Most newspapers of the 1800s were linked to a particular political party, and their content reflected those biases as well as the biases of society. It was not unusual, therefore, for journalists to display explicit racial bias. One such example was adventure writer Jack London, who covered boxing for the *New York Herald*. London began campaigning for a Jeffries-Johnson match as soon as Johnson defeated Tommy Burns. "Jim Jeffries must now emerge from his alfalfa farm and remove that golden smile from Jack Johnson's face," London wrote in 1908.[5]

The fight deal included a purse valued at more than $2.5 million in today's money.

Anticipation of the match had built to a fever pitch by the time it happened in summer 1910. The same white journalists calling for Jeffries to save the sport were relentless in their assault on Johnson. "If the black man wins, thousands and thousands of his ignorant brothers will misinterpret his victory," wrote the *New York Times* shortly before the fight.[3] A writer for *Collier's* magazine even penned of Jeffries, "Let's hope he kills the coon."[4] *Coon*, a racial slur born during the time of slavery, was used to depict black people as slow and lazy.

Foreign journalists also began to comment on the uniquely racist nature of the fight. One French sportswriter expressed his concern that the event might lead to even more hatred of black people in the United States.

More than 16,000 spectators gathered to witness the fight in an open-air stadium in Reno, Nevada. Fifteen rounds later, Johnson was the undisputed world champion. The stunned, mostly white crowd slipped away in near silence after Johnson's victory. Almost immediately, telegraphs and phones spread the news of Johnson's victory around the world. The news led to jubilant celebrations as well as angry demonstrations and race-driven brawls. As newspapers around the country published their reports, Johnson looked forward to more respect and more freedom to live as the successful man he was. Unfortunately, those dreams were not to be.

ARREST AND CONVICTION

Throughout his career, Johnson had taken special pride in forcing white sportswriters to acknowledge his victories. This time was no exception. Yet some of the journalists also scolded Johnson for daring to think of himself as better than whites. "Your place in the world is just what it was," wrote the Los Angeles Times after Johnson defeated Jeffries.[6]

America's dominant white culture could not arrange a defeat for Johnson in the boxing ring. It could, however, find another way to remind him of his place in the world. In November 1912, Johnson was arrested and charged with violating the White Slave Traffic Act, or Mann Act. This vaguely worded law said that no one could transport

Johnson and his wife, Irene, spent much of their time in Europe.

women across state lines or national boundaries for "prostitution or debauchery" and "other immoral purposes." Historians agree Johnson's arrest and subsequent prison time were not about the Mann Act at all. Rather, they were about the way Johnson lived, what he said, and what he did in a time when black people were expected to be submissive to white people.

Johnson served ten months in federal prison for his conviction. After his release, he fought occasionally, wrote two memoirs, and became an entertainer in vaudeville and carnival acts. He died in an automobile accident in 1946.

In 2004, documentary filmmaker Ken Burns began a campaign for a presidential pardon of Johnson. Sylvester Stallone, actor and star of the boxing movie *Rocky*, joined in the campaign by sharing Johnson's story with President Donald J. Trump. In May 2018, Trump granted that pardon.

Johnson was among the first black athletes to receive widespread coverage in the media. His victories came at a time when racial divides turned what should have been a sporting event into a discussion of race and society. More than 100 years after Johnson captured the world heavyweight title, sports headlines continue to reflect racial issues.

DISCUSSION STARTERS

- Johnson's victory over Jeffries resulted in fights, riots, and confrontations between black people and white people around the world after the match. Have you ever protested the outcome of an event? If so, why?

- Do you think you would have pardoned Johnson if you were president? Why or why not?

- Many white people at the turn of the century feared that Johnson's behavior would upset the social order of the time. Do you see any current social orders as being threatened today? Do you think this change is positive or negative? Why?

CHAPTER TWO

SPORTS JOURNALISM AND THE BLACK PRESS

S ports journalism in the United States began in the 1820s and 1830s with specialized publications focused on boxing and horse racing. The segregation common in the United States at this time, however, meant that these publications covered white athletes almost exclusively. As with the rest of the mainstream press, white sports journalists all but ignored the lives of black athletes, including black boxers and black jockeys.

The few exceptions to this rule were when black boxers or black jockeys competed in matches or races that had cultural and news value as well as sporting interest. Jack Johnson's widely publicized world heavyweight championship fight in 1910 was one of these rare instances of black athlete coverage in the white media. For the same cultural reasons, a race between a horse from the North ridden by a white jockey and a horse from the South ridden by a black jockey might be covered not because of the sporting value but rather because of the North-vs.-South angle.

In the early 1800s, a handful of white US newspapers, including the *New York Post*, the *Charleston Courier*, and the *Richmond Enquirer*, included sports stories in their coverage. By the 1820s and 1830s, more newspapers were carrying

Two black employees work in the composing room at the Richmond Planet.

sports stories, though they again tended to cover those stories from the standpoint of cultural events as opposed to local games and matches. In addition, they covered these stories when they involved predominantly white athletes.

Sports coverage in white newspapers received a major push in the 1830s and 1840s with the advent of the penny press. The penny press was the brainchild of American printer Benjamin Day, who started a newspaper called the *Sun* in New York City. It cost just one penny per copy. At that time, most newspapers were selling for six cents per copy, which made them too expensive for many working-class readers. Day's innovation helped more people get the news of the day and, perhaps more importantly, provided an audience for the advertisements Day sold to pay for producing the paper.

The penny press changed the type of information that was typically included in newspapers. Among those changes was an increase in coverage of sporting events. Day and other penny press publishers realized that their white working-class audience enjoyed reading about sports as well as traditional news. That demand created a need for writers who specialized in writing sports stories.

ENTER THE BLACK PRESS

Just as white sports journalism evolved alongside its editorial counterpart, so, too, did the black sports press continue to change. The black press, defined as newspapers written by and for black people, began in 1827 with a single publication in New York. More than 40 black newspapers were in circulation by the time of the Civil War, and the black press reached the height of its success in the 1920s and 1930s.

The black press flourished at a time when most major newspapers would not run the obituary of a black person, let alone print a news story about a living one. Nor would the mainstream press hire black sportswriters or black journalists. The black press thus stepped in to cover everything from community news and employment opportunities to politics, entertainment, and sports. It also created an outlet for the writing and opinions of not only America's leading black intellects and activists but also aspiring black journalists and black sportswriters.

Among the most well known of these newspapers were the *Defender* of Chicago, Illinois, and the *Courier* of Pittsburgh, Pennsylvania. Editorials in these publications advocated for fair employment, voting rights, and quality schools. All of these issues and more would become the platform for the national civil rights agenda.

A PLACE FOR BLACK ATHLETES

Sports coverage in the black press necessarily followed the evolution of sport in the lives of black people. In the post–Civil War era, black athletes primarily participated in two sports: boxing and baseball.

Boxing attracted black athletes because it seemed to promise more of a fair shake. Boxers won or lost based on their own skills and stamina. In addition, boxing was one of the few ways black people could improve their station in life. Winning fights meant earning money in addition to the admiration of fight fans. Regardless of color, no one could argue that an athlete who owned homes, cars, and fine clothes was not a success. Prominent black boxers such as Jack Johnson were an inspiration to other black athletes. These athletes saw that winning fights led to the respect denied them by Jim Crow laws.

The other sport open to early black athletes was baseball. Baseball began as an amateur sport with all-white teams, all-black teams, and some integrated teams. By the 1890s, black players largely were excluded from professional teams and were completely absent by the turn of the

Chief Bender won 212 games during his major-league career.

century. They formed and played on all-black teams instead. This led to the formation of all-black leagues, the most successful of which were the Negro National League in 1933 and the Negro American League in 1937.

Native American players faced racial slurs in the early days of baseball, yet they were afforded more opportunities to play. Louis Sockalexis, a member of the Penobscot tribe in Maine, joined the Cleveland Spiders in 1897. Among the most famous Native American players is Charles "Chief" Bender. A standout pitcher for 16 seasons, 12 of those with the Philadelphia Athletics, Bender was the son of a Chippewa mother and a German father. He went on to be inducted into the National Baseball Hall of Fame in 1953.

BLACK SPORTS JOURNALISTS

In 1937, the *Courier* caught the eye of a young would-be baseball player named Wendell Smith. Smith had wanted to play professional baseball, but the Detroit Tigers refused to give him a contract because he was black. Smith decided to dedicate his career to sports writing instead and possibly help integrate sports that way. In 1948, Smith became the first black sports journalist to work for a white-owned newspaper when he took a job with the *Herald-American* of Chicago.

Two other early black journalists also played an important role in advancing black athletes through their careers as sports journalists. Joe Bostic was an on-air announcer for Negro League games and sports editor of *People's Voice*, a weekly paper that was widely read by black readers. Bostic went on to become the first black journalist admitted to the Boxing Writers and Track

Writers associations. In addition, he became the first black announcer to be licensed as a ringside announcer at a number of boxing venues. He also became the main ringside boxing announcer at New York's famed Madison Square Garden.

Sam Lacy was another prominent black sports journalist. Lacy wrote for the *Washington Tribune* and the *Defender* and, beginning in 1943, was the sports editor and columnist for a group of black newspapers based in Baltimore. Lacy became the first black member of the Baseball Writers Association of America. His pioneering work has also been recognized in the Baseball Hall of Fame.

By this time in history, black athletes were beginning to have their own voice in the form of the black press. Yet as events quickly showed, their treatment in the white press was less than fair and balanced.

DISCUSSION STARTERS

- Do you think of sports journalists in the same light as journalists covering breaking news? Why or why not?
- The black press played an important role in the struggle for civil rights during the Jim Crow era. How do you think the coverage of black athletes in the black press affected that struggle?
- Segregation in the United States meant that white sports reporters almost exclusively covered stories involving white athletes. How do you think the omission of coverage of black athletes among white readers affected how white people felt about black people?

CHAPTER THREE

CONTRASTS IN COVERAGE

Innovations during the Industrial Revolution made news gathering and printing even more affordable for both the white and black presses. As newspapers grew in size, sporting coverage increased as well due to its popularity with readers. Joseph Pulitzer's *New York World* introduced the sports department in 1883. William Randolph Hearst's *New York Journal* rolled out a dedicated sports section in 1895. By 1892, every major white newspaper had a sports editor on staff.

The manner in which these journalists covered sporting events also changed over the years. It became standard procedure to attend the games, take notes, and interview coaches and players after the game. *New York Evening Sun* journalist Joe Vila became the first reporter to use a typewriter ringside when he covered the boxing match between James Corbett and Tom Sharkey in 1898. Over time, journalists switched from sending their stories via telegram to using telephones and later, computers.

These changes led to many more sports stories and tales of many more athletes. What did not change was the difference between the coverage of white athletes and black athletes by white sports journalists. Black athletes continued to be absent from the pages of white sports sections, with very few exceptions. One of those happened in 1908, when black sprinter John Taylor became the first black man to win an Olympic gold medal for the United States. He was recognized in the press again after his untimely death just four months later.

More than any other sporting event, the Olympics challenged American perceptions of race in sports. The Olympics forced the world to acknowledge athletes of color as Americans first. As such, it required another Olympics to bring any substantial coverage of black athletes into America's white sports press in the early 1900s.

THE ENEMY OF MY ENEMY

The 1936 Summer Olympics in Berlin were as much a cultural clash as a sporting event. At the time, Germany was under the control of Adolf Hitler and the Nazi Party. Hitler hoped the games would showcase the superiority of the white race.

JIM THORPE AND NATIVE AMERICAN BIAS

At the 1912 Olympics, baseball, football, and track-and-field standout Jim Thorpe became the first athlete ever to win gold in both the pentathlon and the decathlon. His record-breaking performance earned him the unofficial title of the world's greatest athlete.

Thorpe was of Native American descent, a fact that was frequently highlighted in media coverage of his accomplishments. It was not until he was seen as an American competitor in the Olympics that reporters began to refer to him more as an individual rather than as a member of the Native American race.

PRIDE OVER POLITICS

Sports has historically provided a neutral alternative to politically and ideologically charged editorial news coverage. While members of a community may have very different viewpoints on controversial issues, virtually everyone can agree on supporting the local ball club or high school sports team. Many sporting events, such as the Olympic games, are even marketed as a chance to bring together all the people of a particular nation despite their differences. For those reasons, events that raise racial or political issues during sports events can be highly controversial.

One example of this occurred during the 1968 Olympics. Black Olympians Tommie Smith and John Carlos made international headlines when they raised their fists during their Olympic medal ceremony to protest human rights violations. More recently, the #TakeAKnee movement in the National Football League (NFL) has used game broadcasts to protest racism in the United States. The strong reactions to both of these protests underscore the historic role of sports as a community where everyone came together in harmony.

Meanwhile, most Americans, including American sports journalists, opposed Hitler.

Jesse Owens and 17 other black American athletes (including two black women) traveled with Team USA to Nazi-controlled Germany. There, they dominated the track-and-field events, winning 14 medals, or one-quarter of the 56 medals won by the entire US team. American journalists were quick to cite the performance of the black athletes as a reason to discredit Hitler's racist views.

Defeating the common enemy, Hitler, helped Jesse Owens gain limited acceptance among the sporting public. White Americans were forced to choose between their racial biases and their hatred of Nazis. Most of the time, their hatred of Nazis won out. Yet in the press, rarely were the accomplishments of Owens and his black teammates mentioned without also bringing up their race.

REPORTING ON RACE

Owens grew up in a sharecropper's shanty. He went on to fame at the 1936 Summer Olympics while he was still a student at Ohio State University. Legendary sportswriter Grantland Rice compared Owens's performance in Berlin to "a wild Zulu running amuck." The writer made similar comments about Owens's black teammates Archie Williams, Cornelius Johnson, and John Woodruff. "The Negroes are just better runners and jumpers," Rice wrote. "Easily, almost lazily and minus any show of extra effort, they have turned sports' greatest spectacle into 'the Black Birds of 1936.'"[1] In addition to reinforcing stereotypes, Rice's writings showed that he continually regarded the black athletes as something other than true Americans.

Black female Olympians faced even greater challenges. Sprinters Tidye Pickett and Louise Stokes made the US track-and-field team in 1936 after being removed from the 1932 team and replaced by slower white runners. Media coverage of Pickett in 1932 exemplified what was then standard treatment of black female athletes.

The 1936 US women's track team prepares to board the SS Manhattan *for the journey to the Berlin Olympics. Tidye Pickett is in the front row, third from right, while Louise Stokes is in the back row at the far right.*

Pickett, a Chicago resident, had tied the national indoor record for the 60-yard dash. The *Chicago Tribune* reported on the accomplishment with the headline "New Playground Star Ties National 60 Yard Record."[2] While Pickett was indeed a star member of a local board of education's playground track team, the article featured a photo of a white woman. In contrast, a black press headline from the *Chicago Defender* read "Nation's Track Stars Bid for Olympics: Tidye Pickett, a Chicago Girl, Equals Record."[3]

Typical of the era, Rice's coverage of the Olympics was highly descriptive and stylized. Sportswriters in the 1920s and 1930s worked to create excitement among readers using fancy prose and visual imagery. Despite that verbose style, Rice and other white journalists rarely addressed the talents and personal character of the black athletes, nor the prejudices they had to overcome to perform as they did on the Olympic stage.

Despite their heroics in Berlin, the US black athletes faced discrimination and segregation upon their return. Silver medalist Mack Robinson, whose younger brother Jackie would one day integrate Major League Baseball (MLB), returned to his home of Pasadena, California, and took a job working for the city. He recalls wearing his Olympic sweatshirt while he pushed a broom cleaning streets. When a judge ordered all Pasadena public swimming pools to be desegregated, city officials retaliated. They fired all black workers, including Robinson.

One of the few black athletes working professionally in the 1930s was boxing legend Joe Louis.

HARD ON THE FIELD. HARDER OFF.

Regardless of the sport, black athletes in America faced more challenges than their white counterparts. Even many coaches acknowledged that black athletes had to be not only incredibly talented on the field but also extra resilient. University of Michigan football coach Harry Kipke ordered his white players to test black athletes trying out for the team by playing extra rough against them. "If, at the end of the week, he doesn't turn in his uniform, then I know I've got a great player," Kipke said.[4]

Joseph Louis Barrow began fighting professionally in 1934 at a time when there were virtually no black athletes in any high-profile American sport. Born in 1914 in Alabama to a sharecropper and a laundress, Louis was the grandson of formerly enslaved people. He quickly made a name for himself with his lightning speed and powerful punches. In 1937, he became the first black boxer since Jack Johnson to hold the world heavyweight title.

Like Johnson before him, Louis was subjected to the racial prejudices and biased media coverage of the time. A reporter at the *Birmingham News* wrote that the boxer was a "tan-skinned throwback to the creature of primitive swamps who gloried in battles and blood."[5] Writing about Louis, Rice described the heavyweight as a "brown cobra" and "a black panther stalking his prey." He likened Louis's speed to "the speed of the jungle" and the "instinctive speed of the wild."[6]

Rice was one of many white sportswriters who attributed the success of black athletes to instincts as opposed to hard work. Other journalists were less kind. Conservative columnist Westbrook Pegler called Louis "the colored boy" and "a cotton-field Negro." Sports columnist Bill Corum wrote of Louis, "He's a big, superbly built Negro youth who was born to listen to jazz music, eat a lot of fried chicken, play ball with the gang on the corner, and never do a lick of heavy work he could escape."[7]

Joe Louis raises his right arm in victory after defeating German rival Max Schmeling in 1938.

Unlike Johnson, Louis offered a carefully crafted image to a world that cared little about the lives of everyday black Americans. His managers presented him as a clean-cut country boy still devoted to his mother and wide eyed with success in the big city. It made him a perfect American foil to Germany's Max Schmeling, whose increasingly close ties to the Nazis made him a villain in the eyes of many Americans. Louis became as much of a hero as a black athlete could be at that time when he defeated Schmeling by knockout in the first round of their 1938 match.

THE STORY BEHIND THE STORY

The Berlin Olympics represented the first time a sporting event had been shown on television. It was not widely viewed, as few people had television sets at that time.

Hall of Famer Joe Morgan, right, *became a prominent color commentator on ESPN's baseball broadcasts.*

After the Berlin Olympics, the next live television broadcast of a sporting event was a college baseball game in 1939.

Radio broadcasts of sporting events had begun in 1921 with the first live voice coverage of a boxing match. Radio broadcasts continued to increase in popularity through the 1920s and 1930s. Television became a popular medium for sports coverage in the 1950s and 1960s. In 1979, the cable network ESPN launched 24-hour sports coverage. All of these developments expanded the volume of sports media and changed the nature of that coverage.

Broadcast media allowed journalists to provide more than simple play-by-play descriptions. Increasingly, they added interviews of coaches and players. However, when there were no coaches of color, or when journalists could only interview white players due to segregation rules, their stories reflected that situation.

Sports journalists also worked to differentiate their coverage from that of their competitors. They worked to find the stories behind the games, the players, and the coaches. Focusing only on the stories of white athletes meant that many important aspects not only of sports but also of the experience of being a person of color in America were not covered.

DISCUSSION STARTERS

- The black press came to be because mainstream newspapers refused to cover most news and events involving black people. Are there populations that the mainstream media ignores today? Which ones? What do you think could be done to change this?

- Prior to television, sportswriters worked to bring the excitement of an athletic event to readers who could not otherwise experience it. How do you think that might change how an event was reported?

- White newspapers referred to Olympic athlete Tidye Pickett as a "playground star." What message did that send to young women of color?

CHAPTER FOUR

BREAKING THE COLOR BARRIER

The integration of professional sports helped usher in more mainstream media coverage of America's black athletes. Despite those gains, the nature of that coverage would continue to reflect the deeply held stereotypes and racial divides within American society.

The black press can take much of the credit for one of the first integrations in professional sports—that of Major League Baseball in 1947. The Brooklyn Dodgers signed Jackie Robinson, a black athlete recommended to general manager Branch Rickey by black press journalist Wendell Smith, in 1945. Smith had been working for years to get MLB to sign a black player. As a journalist at the *Pittsburgh Courier*, he was encouraged to write stories related to civil rights. One of his first such pieces investigated the segregation of Major League Baseball. In 1939, Smith interviewed more than 50 baseball players and managers. He asked for their thoughts on integrating baseball and how they would feel about playing with a black teammate.

More than three-quarters of the people Smith interviewed said they had no problem working with black players. However, when Smith arranged for tryouts of black players for several major league teams in 1945, the owners still refused to sign any of them. Likewise, black sports journalists Joe Bostic and Sam Lacy also advocated for integration. Bostic brought two Negro League players to the Brooklyn Dodgers' spring training camp. Neither received a contract. As early as 1940, Sam Lacy sought a meeting with MLB commissioner Kenesaw Mountain Landis to press for integration of the sport. The commissioner never answered his letters.

INTEGRATING FOOTBALL

Like baseball, football also became integrated in the late 1940s. The National Football League (NFL) was formed in the early 1920s. A few black athletes, including Robert Marshall and Fred Slater, played for those early teams.

Yet in 1933, the last remaining black players were released from the league. From that point on until the league was reintegrated, owners denied the existence of a color ban.

Kenny Washington was a football and baseball standout at the University of California, Los Angeles (UCLA), where he was a teammate of Jackie Robinson. Washington became the first UCLA athlete to be named an All-American. Even Robinson referred to Washington as "the greatest football player I have ever seen."[2] Both the black press and the West Coast mainstream press expressed their outrage when Washington was slighted in postseason honors and denied entry into the professional league. NBC broadcaster Sam Balter openly criticized the league and challenged league owners to publicly state why they had refused to sign someone who was clearly the best football player in the nation at the time. He received no response.

Banned from the segregated NFL, Washington became the biggest star and best player on two West Coast minor league teams. Meanwhile, both the black and white press began to chip away at the apparent unwritten rule that was keeping black talent out of the NFL. Wendell Smith wrote of his disappointment when the All-America Football Conference (AAFC), a fledgling competitor to the NFL that was formed in 1944, also ignored black players, including Washington. Even some white fans joined in calling for an end to the ban.

UCLA halfback Kenny Washington went on to integrate the NFL with the help of two black journalists.

The press pressure ultimately paid off when two pro football teams sought to use the Los Angeles Memorial Coliseum. Black writers Halley Harding and Herman Hill objected to allowing any organization that practiced racial discrimination to use the stadium. Under that pressure, the Los Angeles Rams of the NFL signed Washington in March 1946. One Rams coach even acknowledged that the decision was made so the team could use the stadium, meaning integration likely would not have happened had the Rams not recently moved from Cleveland, Ohio, where they already had a stadium. Back in Ohio, however, the AAFC's Cleveland Browns signed two black players later that year. Coach and part owner Paul Brown ignored the implicit color ban and instead stated his intent to sign the best athletes, regardless of color.

The final NFL team to sign a black player was the Washington Redskins. It remained a segregated team until 1962. While MLB annually celebrates its desegregation on April 15, the NFL has no corresponding event.

THE GREATEST

By the early 1960s, MLB, the NFL, and the National Basketball Association (NBA), which integrated in 1950, had all signed black athletes. Black tennis star Althea Gibson had been victorious at Wimbledon. The National Collegiate Athletic Association (NCAA) had fielded integrated basketball teams. It was a time of change and increased activism for civil rights. It also was the beginning of the career of boxer Cassius Clay.

Clay burst onto the national scene by winning a gold medal in boxing at the 1960 Rome Olympics. He became the world heavyweight champion in 1964 after taking the title from Sonny Liston. Jackie Robinson was quoted as saying Clay "might just be one of the greatest heavyweight champions this country has ever produced."[3]

The white sports media was by this time more willing to cover the accomplishments of black athletes. Yet both mainstream and black press reporters were unsure what to make of the boxer who announced after the Liston victory that he was converting to Islam and changing his name to

HOWARD COSELL AND MUHAMMAD ALI

White broadcaster Howard Cosell was among the biggest defenders of Muhammad Ali when the heavyweight champion refused induction into the military for religious reasons in 1967. The two developed an on-air rapport that delighted audiences and boosted ratings even as they addressed not only boxing but also the hot-button issues of the late 1960s and early 1970s. Cosell's support was not without personal cost, however. His daughter reported that the family received telephoned threats at their house calling Cosell nasty names and denigrating him for his close relationship to a black man.

Muhammad Ali used his victories in the ring to call attention to racism. Yet not all black athletes have been comfortable in the role of activist. Michael Jordan was for years among the most successful athletes in the National Basketball Association. Jordan also was a successful businessman. In 2017, he had an estimated net worth of $1.3 billion and generated an estimated $110 million in annual revenue from his athletic shoe promotion agreement with Nike.[4] Jordan came under fire in 1990 for refusing to endorse a Democratic political candidate seeking to unseat a Republican senator widely regarded as racist. Jordan was reported to have said about his refusal, "Republicans buy sneakers, too."[5]

Jordan broke his silence in 2016 and spoke out about athletes protesting racial injustice. "Those who exercise the right to peacefully express themselves should not be demonized or ostracized," he said.[6]

Muhammad Ali. The *New York Times* took five years before it would refer to him as Ali.

SPORTS ILLUSTRATED SPEAKS UP

The civil rights movement encouraged more research into issues of racism and discrimination. Sports media was not immune. A study of coverage of black basketball players in *Sports Illustrated* revealed a pattern of omission. The research determined that the dramatic growth in black athletes in Division I college basketball between 1954 and 1986 was not accurately reflected in the publication, which remains one of America's leading sports magazines. Researchers found that "in proportion to their population and their performances on court, black basketball athletes received far fewer articles than their contributions to the sport seem to warrant."[7] In addition, the researchers found a 30-year gap between the magazine's first and second covers featuring female black athletes.

However, *Sports Illustrated* did take an early step toward covering race issues in sports with a series of articles in 1968. Managing editor Andre Laguerre kept his plans for the features a secret from the *Sports Illustrated* management for fear that the series would be scuttled if word leaked out. "The Black Athlete—A Shameful Story," became the magazine's most-read series since it had been founded 14 years earlier. An editorial in the magazine summed up the conviction that drove Laguerre and writer Jack Olsen to create the series. "We felt there no longer was room for the complacency that until now has characterized the world of sport."[8]

DISCUSSION STARTERS

- Wendell Smith wrote about both sports and civil rights issues for the *Pittsburgh Courier*. How did those two issues intersect in the 1940s? How do you think they intersect today?

- Why do you think the NFL maintained that it had no ban on black players even though its teams refused to sign black players?

- Muhammad Ali became one of the most outspoken athletes of all time. How do you think his actions influenced the connection between sports and celebrity?

VOICES
OF CHANGE

Early black journalists such as Sam Lacy, Wendell Smith, and Joe Bostic were important voices working to improve the perceptions and treatment of black athletes in Jim Crow America. Journalism has changed significantly since those days, yet the voices of black sports journalists continue to press for change. Here are some of the standouts:

Stuart Scott was a longtime anchor of ESPN's signature *SportsCenter* show. He was hired in 1993 to improve ESPN's appeal with younger viewers, and he accomplished that and more with such signature phrases as "Boo-yah!" Scott died in 2015 after a long battle with cancer.

Pam Oliver caught the attention of both ESPN and Fox Sports for her game knowledge and interviewing skills. She has worked on the sidelines of both the NFL and NBA playoffs after beginning her journalism career as a reporter in Georgia.

Michael Wilbon's career spans print, radio, television, and new media. He has cohosted the popular ESPN show *Pardon the Interruption* since 2001. He is also an NBA studio analyst and in 2017 received the National Press Club's prestigious Fourth Estate Award.

Sage Steele is among the most popular commentators on ESPN, serving as the lead host for *SportsCenter on the Road*. Steele began her career in 1995 as a television producer and reporter in Indiana, eventually moving up to NASCAR and the IndyCar Series. She joined Fox Sports in 2000 and ESPN in 2007.

CHAPTER FIVE

BLACK BRAWN AND WHITE BRAIN

B lack people in America historically have been subjected to negative and misleading generalizations. In his book *From Jack Johnson to LeBron James: Sports, Media, and the Color Line,* author Chris Lamb points to historical generalizations of individuals of African descent as "ignorant, lazy, happy-go-lucky, savage and animal-like."[1] At the same time, black athletes historically have been subject to race-based generalizations. Key among these are that the success of black athletes stems more from natural genetic ability than from intelligence and hard work.

Even individuals who generally support black athletes have been found to harbor some of these stereotypes. Howard Cosell was among the most popular sports commentators on American television in the 1970s and 1980s. On a *Monday Night Football* broadcast in 1983, Cosell referred to Washington Redskins wide receiver Alvin Garrett as "that little monkey."[2] Cosell refused to apologize, citing his strong relationships with many black athletes, including Muhammad Ali, and the fact that he had used the same term previously both for a white athlete and for his own grandson.

In April 1987, Los Angeles Dodgers vice president and general manager Al Campanis was fired after an appearance

Howard Cosell, right, pretends to throw a punch while his friend Muhammad Ali mugs for the cameras in 1981.

on ABC's *Nightline* program. On the show, *Nightline* host Ted Koppel asked Campanis why so few black people were in management jobs in baseball. Campanis replied, "I truly believe they may not have some of the necessities to be a field manager or perhaps a general manager."[3] Campanis went on to state that black people were not adapted to be competitive swimmers, either, due to physical attributes.

One year later, CBS fired sports commentator Jimmy "the Greek" Snyder for saying that black athletes were superior to white athletes because of selective breeding during slavery. MSNBC executives took action when they fired host Don Imus in 2007 after he made derogatory

SHOWTIME VS. FUNDAMENTALS: THE LAKERS-CELTICS RIVALRY

The 1980s featured one of the greatest rivalries in the history of the NBA. Between 1980 and 1989, the Los Angeles Lakers made the NBA Finals eight times and won five championships. Meanwhile, the Boston Celtics reached the NBA Finals five times in that same span, winning three titles. The rivals met in the NBA Finals in 1984, 1985, and 1987.

The Lakers were led by a trio of black stars—point guard Earvin "Magic" Johnson, center Kareem Abdul-Jabbar, and forward James Worthy. The team picked up the nickname "Showtime" for its razzle-dazzle performances, complete with celebrity fans and the famed Laker Girls dancers. The Celtics' star player was Larry Bird, a white forward from a small town in Indiana. The Celtics were viewed as a more blue-collar team playing their games in a musty, no-frills arena. The rivalry often reflected racist stereotypes of white athletes as hard workers and black athletes as naturally gifted. Sportswriters of the time furthered the stereotypes with their characterizations of the teams as "playground style" for the Lakers versus "fundamental basketball" with the Celtics.[5]

comments about the appearance of several black players on the Rutgers women's basketball team.

Frequently, this type of bias can still be found in what might appear to be harmless comments by a sportscaster. A black athlete might "spring off the floor," or demonstrate athleticism, while a white athlete might show "toughness off the bench," or demonstrate mental power. A white athlete might be characterized as "one of the hardest workers," while a black teammate might be the "strong man."[4]

QUANTIFYING BIAS

Racial stereotypes have been widely documented in research that delves into how the sports media has covered white and black athletes. The first major work to explore the differences focused on professional football in the 1970s. The research analyzed broadcasts of NFL games and evaluated comments made by sportscasters. The research found that white football players were more likely to be praised for good plays. At the same time, black players were more likely to be criticized for bad plays.

Furthermore, researchers were able to identify the race of the player based on the comments made. One of the researchers was a blind person and was neither familiar with the players nor could identify the athlete's race visually. However, when asked to predict the race of the athlete based solely on the sports commentary, the blind researcher was consistently able to correctly identify the athlete's race.

Researchers again focused on the NFL 20 years later in evaluating direct comments from broadcasters covering the games. This research found that individual players were described more from an intellectual standpoint when they were white. When the players were black athletes, the comments focused on physical qualities.

Media discussion of former NBA stars Magic Johnson, left, *and Larry Bird exemplified the distorted coverage of race in sports.*

COLOR-CODED COMMENTARY IN COLLEGE

The same researchers turned their focus to collegiate football and basketball in a similar study published in 2005. That research analyzed televised coverage of NCAA football and men's basketball games during the late 1990s. The broadcasts allowed researchers to evaluate live, unscripted, unedited coverage.

The coverage was analyzed according to two categories—a cognitive/intellectual category and a character category. Within the cognitive/intellectual category, researchers evaluated for comments pertaining to either on-field intellect or off-field intellect. Comments on a player's character were evaluated based on what they said about the morality, integrity, and values of a particular player. The study also examined comments related to personal interest stories about players. Researchers also took note of the race of the commenter versus the race of the athlete being discussed.

While most of the broadcasters commenting on the games were white, comments from broadcasters of color were not significantly different from comments of white broadcasters. Likewise, there were no significant differences found between the basketball and football results.

What researchers did find was similar to the results of the NFL study in the 1970s. Announcers continued to discuss black athletes in terms of physical abilities and white athletes in terms of hard work and intellect. The research also determined that bias existed in how sports commentators discussed black athletes as people. Overall, researchers identified 18 negative statements made by commentators about a player's off-field intelligence, character, or a negative personal interest story. All 18 of those incidents involved black athletes. In the same categories, white athletes received only positive comments.

OK ON THE COURT BUT NOT OFF IT

Research such as this points to another form of negative racial bias in media coverage of black athletes. That difference is in how a black player is covered as an athlete and as a person. Any time sports journalists turn their focus off the field, the court, or the ring, it presents an opportunity to tell more of the story of that individual. With that opportunity, however, comes the possibility for reinforcing other racial stereotypes.

Just as researchers evaluated televised game broadcasts for bias regarding "brawn versus brains," so too has the method been used to evaluate other biases. The research found that when it came to comments about an athlete's character, white players received 58 percent of the positive comments recorded. Similarly, white players received 56 percent of the positive comments recorded related to personal interest stories.

Meanwhile, all recorded negative comments in personal interest stories were directed at black athletes. As the commentators moved further from discussing the player as an athlete and closer to discussing the player as a person, recorded negative comments increased for black players and decreased for white players.

BIAS IN PRINT

Broadcast coverage of sports is far from the only venue for racist stereotypes of black athletes. Two separate studies also analyzed coverage of black athletes in *Sports Illustrated* magazine.

The first of the two studies examined *Sports Illustrated*'s MLB coverage from 2000 to 2007. That study found that about 80 percent of the time, articles in the magazine characterized white players as working hard to succeed. Hard work was not featured as a primary factor in the success of black players.

BETTER PLAYERS? OR BETTER PLACES TO PLAY?

Media bias against black basketball players often compares their performance in jumping, speed, and reaction time. One theory for this difference was developed by Donal Carlston. Through an analysis of sports biographies, sports sociology studies, and interviews with basketball players, Carlston formulated a theory stating that these differences in play can be traced to the types of experiences players had in their youth.

According to the theory, black players are more likely to grow up playing against all ages on heavily used urban courts. They must shoot and pass in a way that their more experienced opponents cannot easily predict. Playing with flair can make a player more popular with his peers and thus provide more playing time in pickup games. In contrast, white players frequently learn the game in a more controlled setting with organized teams and coaches leading drills to develop specific skills.

Coverage of the players' personal lives also differed. Articles on white athletes addressed their off-the-field hobbies, physical descriptors, and the role their fathers played in teaching them the game. Coverage of black players' personal lives focused on their backgrounds and families, most commonly referencing their mothers, especially single mothers. Black players also were more commonly featured as having to overcome obstacles, such as proving themselves, than were white players.

THE QUARTERBACK ISSUE

One of the most glaring brains vs. brawn biases in sports can be found in the NFL quarterback position. Recent research indicates this bias may be so prevalent it even affects the perceptions black athletes have of their own abilities.

To test for bias, researchers asked white and black college students to assess write-ups and photos of black and white professional quarterbacks based on four stereotypical descriptors. The descriptors were intelligence,

In 1974, James Harris of the Los Angeles Rams became the first black quarterback to win an NFL playoff game.

physical strength, natural ability, and leadership. Both groups of students assigned the stereotypical descriptors by race—physical strength and natural ability to black players; intelligence and leadership to white players. However, in a surprising turn, the black students stereotyped both races more strongly than the white students.

A second study used a group of white subjects with a wider range of ages and education levels. The group reviewed the same paragraphs and photos. In this group, black stereotypes were assigned to the black players, but white stereotypes were not assigned to the white players. In this group, the study participants avoided assigning white stereotypes to the black quarterbacks even when they were directly told that the black quarterbacks were intelligent or good leaders. Studies such as this raise concerns that stereotypes of black athletes are so strong it is hard for black athletes themselves not to believe them.

BIAS ON THE SIDELINES

In addition to racial bias in sports commentary about athletes, researchers also have reported on bias in the coverage of coaches. A study published in 2010 looked at media coverage of newly hired coaches in NCAA Division I football. The study evaluated the news releases and subsequent reporting on new coaches of color.

Researchers found that black coaches were underrepresented in the hiring process. This was especially evident when comparing the number of black coaching candidates to the number of black players on the teams in question. When schools did hire black coaches, it tended to be only for teams with a high percentage of black players.

A conclusion of the research into black coaches was strikingly similar to the findings in the study of black players. News coverage of new black coaches tended to focus on the ability of those coaches to help their teams by recruiting new players and building relationships with existing players. In contrast, newly hired white coaches were covered from the standpoint of how their knowledge and experience would benefit the team.

DISCUSSION STARTERS

- Black athletes dominate in some sports but not others. What societal reasons can you think of to explain that?

- Research on racism in sports has focused on basketball and football. What examples of racism have you seen in other sports?

- What racial stereotypes have you seen applied to white athletes?

CHAPTER SIX

A TALE OF TWO ATHLETES

T he 1960s were a time of great change in the United States. Professional sports were by now officially integrated, yet there remained two levels of treatment for athletes based on their color.

The Civil Rights Act of 1964 had made discrimination illegal, yet black athletes still found themselves in a different world than their white teammates. In 1965, black players boycotted the American Football League All-Star Game when they were asked to stay in hotel rooms that were not comparable to those of their white teammates. In 1968, black track-and-field athletes refused to participate in the New York Athletic Club's 100th Anniversary meet at Madison Square Garden. Their refusal was to protest that the club excluded black people.

Even today, evaluations of media coverage of black and white athletes indicate the two groups still face different treatment, though in more subtle ways. One of these differences is seen in the way the media treats white subjects versus black subjects in stories that take place off the playing field.

In 2007, Atlanta Falcons quarterback Michael Vick was indicted in federal court on charges of participating in an illegal dogfighting ring. Pittsburgh Steelers quarterback

Ben Roethlisberger was accused of rape in 2008 and again in 2010.

Coverage of the Vick incident included information on his past brushes with the law and other behavior issues. Roethlisberger also had past controversies, yet Vick's were covered more often and in greater detail. Stories about Vick became increasingly negative as the investigation progressed, even though charges had not yet been filed. Stories about Roethlisberger tended to focus on the dubious credibility of his accusers, insinuating that Roethlisberger wasn't the type to be a rapist. Much of the Vick coverage did not address the fact that he hailed from a culture in which dogfighting was an accepted activity. Articles on Roethlisberger discredited his first accuser even as they reported on the second.

Vick was immediately suspended from the NFL and ended up spending 18 months in prison. Roethlisberger served a

HANK AND THE BABE

Babe Ruth was known as a hard drinker who was seen with many different women throughout his career. Unlike with Jack Johnson, reporters largely ignored these activities because "the Babe" was white. When black player Hank Aaron rose from humble beginnings to quietly and diligently approach Ruth's career record of 714 home runs, the racial slurs quickly followed. At one point during Aaron's quest to break the record, he received more than 600 pieces of mail in one day. Sixty percent of those letters spewed racist venom. Aaron triumphed in spite of the hate, ending his career with a total of 755 home runs.

Pittsburgh Steelers quarterback Ben Roethlisberger addresses the media in 2010 after he was cleared of sexual assault charges for the second time in two years.

four-game suspension, but charges were never filed in either case and he returned to quarterback the Steelers. While the allegations against and experiences of the two athletes were very different, they highlight a larger truth. Sports and crime are both popular topics of media coverage. When they cross over, they create headlines. Research also indicates that black athletes and white athletes are portrayed differently in crime reporting.

These findings stem from research that evaluated all articles involving athletes and crimes published in three national newspapers over a three-year period. The study found that black athletes were overrepresented as criminals compared with white athletes. In addition, the crimes of black athletes were discussed in the media in more explicit detail and were associated with more negative consequences than those of white athletes. Finally, crimes involving white athletes tended to focus more on the situation that led to the crime, removing blame from the person who committed it. Crimes involving black athletes tended to put the blame more on the character of the athlete involved.

Another study in 2015 analyzed 155 news articles and showed that white athletes are more likely overall to get coverage in the media—43 percent more coverage than black athletes.[1] At the same time, the study found that black athletes were more likely to get media coverage when a crime had been committed.

ARE NFL PLAYERS MORE LIKELY TO COMMIT CRIMES?

NFL players have made headlines for arrests for such crimes as domestic abuse, drunken driving, and dogfighting. Focusing on headlines alone, it would seem the arrest rate for NFL players is unusually high.

A 2015 study by researchers at the University of Texas at Dallas concluded differently. The research showed the arrest rate for the general population of males age 20 to 39 between 2000 and 2013 was 1.5 to two times as high as that of NFL athletes for most of the years analyzed. One exception was in the area of violent crimes, where NFL players showed a higher arrest rate than the general population for six out of 14 years studied.[2]

SKEWED COVERAGE IN OTHER SPORTS

The high percentage of black players in both the NFL and NBA have made those sports flash points for crime stories involving black athletes. However, traditionally white sports such as golf and tennis have exhibited similar patterns when covering issues that affect athletes away from the field of competition.

Even people who aren't golf fans are aware of Tiger Woods. In 1997, at age 21, Woods became the youngest player ever to win the Masters tournament. His triumph—in a tournament that had barred black people before 1975, at a club that had no black members before 1990—made international headlines. So, too, did his 2009 sex scandal.

Far fewer people are aware of Dustin Johnson's third failed drug test in 2014. One of the top players in golf, Johnson, who is white, had tested positive for cocaine use and took a "voluntary leave of absence" from the tour before being suspended for six months.

While no crime was involved, critics have pointed to *USA Today*'s revelation of black tennis star Arthur Ashe's health concerns as another example of racism in sports media. Ashe was bullied by the paper into going public with the fact that he was HIV positive, likely the result of a blood transfusion.

Ashe was retired at the time of the revelation by *USA Today*. However, he remained active in many causes and thus was still a public figure. In today's increasingly connected world, white and black athletes alike must manage the dual challenges of performance and celebrity, even as racism creeps in.

DISCUSSION STARTERS

- Do you believe Michael Vick was treated fairly? Why or why not?
- Do you think people who read or watch sports news play a role in encouraging biased reporting of athletes? If yes, how?
- Publishers and broadcasters are seeking more diversity in their sports-reporting ranks to create stories that more accurately reflect the interests of their readers and viewers. Which sports stories would you like to see that are not currently being covered?

CHAPTER SEVEN

SOCIAL MEDIA: THE NEW HEAVYWEIGHT

S ports have always been nearly as much about the fans as about the players. Sportswriters have worked not only to share what happens on the playing field but also to do it in a way that engages and excites sports fans.

For most of the history of professional sports, sports journalists have been in control of the message. Printed newspapers and magazines were the primary sources of sports information prior to the 1990s. The first sports web log (later known as a blog) appeared in 1991. By 2004, printed news ranked last in terms of the preferred news source for sports fans. Fans began taking over their own news feeds and sharing, and in 2013, fans sent more than 490 million tweets about sports alone.[1]

While 54 percent of sports journalists also use Twitter to report, social media has changed the dynamics of who says what to whom.[2] Thanks to Facebook, Twitter, YouTube, and Instagram, sports fans can have followings the same as sportswriters.

Athletes now can cultivate an individual social media presence and control the message about their own performance and character. For black athletes in particular, this has allowed them to better control misinformation, bias, or lack of information altogether. Sometimes athletes respond directly to fans. Twitter in particular has become a favorite platform for sports fans viewing televised events to express their thoughts in real time.

Unlike traditional journalists, sports fans on social media are not held to ethical codes of impartiality, balanced reporting, or fact-checking. Journalists must not only verify the accuracy of sporting reports but also of sporting fans if they wish to use the same information. Social media also has made it easy for fans to comment—positively or negatively—on journalistic coverage of sports on social media. Finally, social media has made everyone a reporter, whether they have the credentials or not. Unofficial reporters now have the same opportunity as the official ones to comment very publicly on games and athletes.

MORE FANS ADDING SOCIAL MEDIA TO THEIR SPORTING EXPERIENCES

If Super Bowl 50 and soccer's World Cup are any indication, sports and social media are a perfect fit for each other. Pre-event surveys of US consumers found that 65 percent were planning to be on Facebook while watching Super Bowl 50 in 2016. In addition, 25 percent of respondents said they planned to use Twitter, and 18 percent were planning to use Instagram.

Globally, the 2014 World Cup earned top honors in an analysis of Facebook interactions for sporting events through May 2017. That event, which ran from June 12 through July 13, resulted in some three billion interactions on the social media site. The 2016 Rio Olympic Games were a distant second with 1.5 billion Facebook interactions.[3]

SORE LOSERS, RACIST TWEETS

In the 2012 National Hockey League (NHL) playoffs, Joel Ward, a black player for the Washington Capitals, scored a dramatic, game-winning goal in overtime against the Boston Bruins in Boston. The goal clinched the series for the Capitals, knocking Boston out of the playoffs. It also led to an almost immediate tirade of racial slurs against Ward on Twitter.

Sportswriter Ian Carey of the *Huffington Post* covered the incident. "These hockey fans seemingly had no inhibitions of posting their racist language for the whole world to see," he wrote. He noted that some fans had referred to hockey as a "white man's game" and even told Ward to "go play basketball." Carey noted that while the small group of people posting inappropriately on Twitter

Washington Capitals player Joel Ward saw the ugly side of social media after he scored an important goal against Boston.

was not representative of hockey fans in general, it was nonetheless troubling. "It is disturbing that so many people felt that posting such comments was somehow OK," he wrote.[4]

HERO OR THUG?

Twitter again became a platform for hate speech in January 2014. In the final seconds of the National Football Conference (NFC) Championship Game, Seattle Seahawks cornerback Richard Sherman deflected a pass in the end zone to win the game and send the Seahawks to the Super Bowl. Sherman then gave an interview to Fox Sports reporter Erin Andrews.

During the intensely emotional interview, Sherman yelled and proclaimed that he was the NFL's best cornerback. Shortly after the interview aired, Twitter lit up with racial slurs and other negative responses to Sherman's interview. Among other things, fans called Sherman an ape and a thug. Sherman responded on Twitter that the negative comments were further evidence of racism in America.

An analysis of 100 Twitter posts related to the Sherman interview found several themes. Most fans regarded Sherman's behavior during the interview as hostile instead of fired up after a big win. There were more racist tweets the day of the interview than the day following, with "thug" showing up as a common term. Finally, the day after the interview, more fans stepped up to defend Sherman. A common theme became Sherman's academic record, including his 3.9 grade point average at Stanford University.

Richard Sherman, left, was accused of being a thug after giving an emotional interview to Erin Andrews of Fox Sports.

Reaction among traditional sports journalists was likewise mixed. Some criticized Sherman for a lack of class in the interview, while others approved of his refreshing approach in lieu of the standard postgame clichés most players and coaches provide.

THE DOWNSIDE OF SUPERFANS

Racist online comments are hardly exclusive to sports. Black athletes, however, might be more susceptible than other public figures because of the nature of sports and sports fans. Some research into avid sports fans indicates that they

HASHTAG ADVOCACY

In February 2018, NBA star LeBron James spoke about family, personal growth, and the challenges of being a black person during an ESPN interview. Shortly after the interview aired, Fox News broadcaster Laura Ingraham criticized James on her show for talking about politics. "Keep the political comments to yourselves," she said of James and other athletes speaking up about politics and racism. "Shut up and dribble."[5]

James responded with an Instagram post and the hashtag #wewillnotshutupanddribble. The hashtag quickly went viral on Instagram and Twitter as it was picked up by James' fans along with civil rights supporters.

James' protests against racism resurfaced in June 2018 during the NBA Finals pitting his Cavaliers against the Golden State Warriors. Despite their rivalry, James and Warriors star Stephen Curry agreed that neither team would make a White House visit if it were victorious. Their decision came in the wake of the Trump administration's criticism of professional athletes protesting racism.

become more emotionally invested when watching sports than do casual fans. In addition, researchers have found that closely identifying with a particular sports team enables individuals to feel they are part of something bigger, which helps them feel better about themselves.

When a fan identifies so closely with a team, it is hard for that fan to attribute the loss to anything his or her team might have done. Rather, it is easier to attribute the loss to the other team. In Ward's case, some Boston fans took out their ire on their opponent rather than blaming their own team for the loss. Existing stereotypes and biases of some fans then added a racist nature to an already disappointing experience.

The United States is not the only place where athletes have been targeted by racist fan comments on social media. European soccer has also been rocked by racist tweets from fans. In one instance, a fan who sent a hate tweet was sentenced to 56 days in jail. The tweet was posted after black soccer star Fabrice Muamba collapsed during a game after suffering a heart attack. Muamba was receiving medical care on the field when the negative tweets began.

As with any media, social media has both helped and harmed athletes of color. While racism has more opportunities now due to ever more voices, there are also more opportunities to raise awareness and create change.

DISCUSSION STARTERS

- Do you think sports fans should be able to say whatever they want about athletes on social media? When does it become hate speech?

- When you're watching a live event, do you follow along on social media, too? Do fans' observations make those of sports journalists less important?

- Many athletes use social media to interact directly with fans—with no middleman such as a reporter. Has following an athlete on his or her social media account ever caused you to think differently about that person?

CHAPTER EIGHT

FRAMING RACISM IN SPORTS MEDIA

S ports traditionally has provided journalists with the opportunity to cover multiple story angles. One story focuses on what is happening on the playing field. The other story focuses on the athlete off the field. Depending on how they are handled, both can be damaging to black athletes.

Sports is one of the few areas within mainstream media in which black people receive a lot of coverage and thus a lot of attention. Black athletes comprise the majority of NFL and NBA rosters, but the same is not true in other high-profile professions.

Less than 14 percent of speaking roles in the top 100 films in 2016 were given to black actors.[1] Black people comprised less than 10 percent of members of the 115th Congress.[2] In early 2018, there were only three Fortune 500 companies led by black chief executive officers (CEOs).[3] So when generalizations are made about black people, they're more informed by the words and actions of athletes than those from other professions.

MAINTAINING STEREOTYPES

At the same time, much of what is said about black athletes is reflective of hundreds of years of stereotypes about black people. A survey conducted by the National Opinion Research Center found that 56 percent of white respondents thought black people were more violent. The same survey found that 62 percent of white people surveyed thought black people were not as hardworking as white people. Finally, more than half of the white people surveyed thought black people were less intelligent than white people.[4]

Research into sports media coverage of black athletes has shown that the stereotypes of black athletes as lazier and less intelligent

SOCIAL MEDIA FOR GOOD: CALLING OUT BIASES

Racist comments by two radio broadcasters during a high school basketball game in northern Iowa ended in their dismissal, thanks in part to social media. The game, in November 2017, pitted Forest City High School against Eagle Grove High School.

During the game, an announcer and a producer made negative comments about the ethnicity of three Latino athletes on the Eagle Grove team. At one point, one of the commentators suggested that the Latino players should "go back where they came from."[5] Clips from the game including the comments were posted on Facebook. The Facebook post drew attention to the issue, resulting in the dismissal of the commentators, one of whom also worked as a grade school teacher. Forest City High School, which hosted the game, also issued an apology.

The US Congress is one of many institutions in the country that suffers from a lack of diversity.

are still found in sports commentary. It is not surprising that surveys continue to find these stereotypes of black people when those same stereotypes are reinforced in the venue where black people are featured most prominently in the media. When sports fans consume their sports media on a regular, repeated basis, as is typically the case with any loyal fan, the stereotypes have multiple opportunities to take root and spread.

PRIMED FOR RACISM

Racism in sports media coverage thus becomes a vicious cycle when the journalists providing the coverage frame issues and interpret behaviors based on racial biases and misperceptions. A color commentator on television may need to fill a minute of live broadcast time with unscripted talk. The pressure that commentator is under may lead him or her to share stories or insights that draw from stereotypes formed early in their lives.

This phenomenon, where the mere presence of black people on a court or a field or in a boxing ring may cause a commentator to share an old bias, is called priming. Regardless of the reason, sharing negative biases with a live television audience reinforces those biases—and potentially the discriminatory behaviors associated with them—and the cycle continues.

THE BLACK ANGLE

Racial biases among sports journalists also impact the way many of those journalists report about athletes off the court. In preparing a story, journalists must determine the key message they want to share in terms of how it might interest their audience. This is called the angle. A single event may have multiple angles, and it is often up to the reporter and editor to choose which angle to present.

Here again, priming comes into play. For example, a reporter who believes black people are more likely to use illegal drugs may seize upon that theme when reporting an incident involving both illegal drugs and gambling, even if the gambling issue was what made the event news initially. In 1991, black boxer Sugar Ray Leonard was involved in a high-profile divorce. Documents pertaining to the case were leaked to the press, and the *Los Angeles Times* published excerpts from the documents. The excerpts included Leonard admitting to abusing drugs and alcohol. At that time, multiple stories in the news had linked black athletes and substance abuse. In the Leonard case, reporters quickly seized upon the drug and alcohol angle regardless of the other issues that were involved in the divorce.

Journalists also control the words used in the story and the facts that are, or are not, brought into it. For example, calling someone an "alleged victim" leads to a different reaction in an audience than calling someone an "accuser." The images included with the story likewise help set the frame. Crime scene photos can create a different perception of an event than smiling photos of suspects from earlier, happier times.

One result of framing is that even though black athletes may continue to experience success on the playing field, they may not be accepted into society once they step off it. This creates a ripple effect that can inhibit the progress of black people in all other aspects of life as well.

LARGE, SCARY BLACK MEN

Black male athletes have experienced discrimination in multiple forms over the years, but one stereotype has been particularly destructive. Research has pointed to a pervasive belief that black men are seen as larger, stronger, and more threatening than white men of the same size.

The research behind these findings used a series of 90 photographs of both black and white men. The photos portrayed high school football players who were being recruited by colleges. The actual heights and weights of the players were available to the researchers, but not to the survey participants. The photos then were evaluated by nonblack volunteers.

The evaluators judged the black athletes as taller and heavier than white athletes who were the same size. Using the same photos, two other studies found that nonblack evaluators regarded the black athletes as stronger and more capable of doing harm. The research team also had a group of black people evaluate the photos. The black people likewise deemed the black men in the photos to be stronger. However, they did not deem them to be any more capable of harm than the white athletes portrayed.

This and other research sheds light on the problem of unconscious bias and how it can be triggered by viewing black men primarily as athletes. Less-common or absent images of black men in the media as fathers, politicians, businessmen, and community leaders also add to this problem.

Black boys grow up with a skewed perception of which career and education options are open to them. They see black athletes far more often than black CEOs, black presidents, or black scientists. This can make them spend more time working on their athletic skills, to the detriment of other workplace skills.

They also must make their way in a world that may see them as people to fear. If people see fear in the eyes of strangers looking at them for the first time, they can question their own value to society and make different choices than they might have under other circumstances.

DISCUSSION STARTERS

o   Journalists are not the only people who frame issues. Politicians, teachers, and parents do as well. When has an issue in your life been framed to try to alter your perception of it?

o   Why are stereotypes harmful even to individuals who do not exemplify them? What are some ways to avoid applying stereotypes?

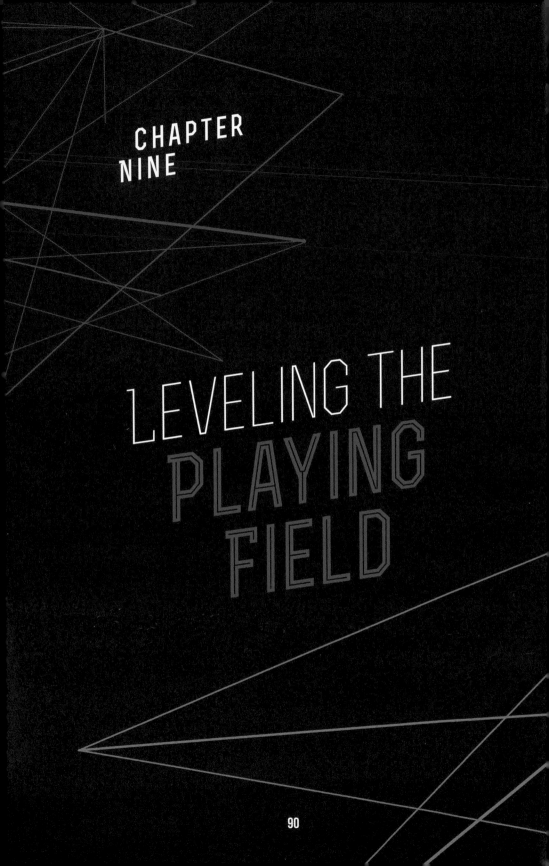

CHAPTER
NINE

LEVELING THE
PLAYING
FIELD

R ecent years have seen slow but steady growth in both the number of sports journalists of color and the number of female sports journalists. In March 1999, a team of researchers wanted to determine whether these developments had had an effect on the level of racial and gender bias in sports coverage.

The researchers analyzed commentary recorded during 66 videotaped basketball games. They concluded that a more diverse pool of sports journalists did have an effect on reducing bias in coverage. While the bias was still present, the more dramatic biases of earlier years were largely gone. Additionally, researchers noted a difference in bias between the more well-known professional announcers, who exhibited less bias, versus the lesser-known announcers, who were responsible for more.

HIGHLIGHTING UNCONSCIOUS BIAS

Researchers also have documented benefits from greater awareness of unconscious bias. An analysis of personal foul calls by NBA referees between 1991 and 2002 suggested that officiating crews were more likely to call fouls on players of the opposite race. This type of bias is called own-race bias. The analysis determined that this level of bias was significant enough to impact the outcomes of games.

The results of this analysis were widely publicized beginning in 2007. NBA stars including Charles Barkley, LeBron James, and Kobe Bryant participated in interviews and discussions on their experiences with the topic. The story was also covered by the *New York Times*, all major news networks, ESPN, and radio talk shows.

Researchers then analyzed officiating calls for both a pre-results period (2003–2006) and a post-results period (2007–2010). Analysts found that officiating crews had stopped making more foul calls on players of the opposite race once the survey results had been widely publicized. This study supports efforts to get more people, including journalists, to talk with people of color about their experiences with bias. When people learn how their biases harm others,

REDUCING UNINTENTIONAL BIAS

Researchers at the University of Wisconsin found a reduction in unintentional bias from a workshop that addresses the issue like a bad habit that can be changed. Psychology professor Patricia Devine and her team created a two-hour workshop that walks participants through the facts on how unintentional bias occurs, what the negative effects of that bias are, and strategies to overcome it. In a 12-week follow-up study, people who had gone through the workshop demonstrated dramatic reductions in racial bias versus those who had not gone through the workshop.

they are more likely to think twice before allowing it to happen again.

ACCOUNTABILITY COUNTS

While overtly racist comments against black athletes by sports commentators have decreased over the years, the industry continues to address several other fronts in the war on bias and racism.

In 2014, the NBA fined LA Clippers owner Donald Sterling $2.5 million and banned him for life from the NBA for asking his then girlfriend not to associate with black people. In June 2016, Fox Sports fired reporter Emily Austen after she made racist remarks about Mexican, Jewish, and Chinese people during a commentary segment. In spring 2017, Denver sportswriter Terry Frei was

TOOLS FOR TRACKING IMPLICIT BIAS

Project Implicit is a long-term research project at Harvard University that enables ordinary individuals to discover biases they don't even know they hold. The program features a variety of online tools aimed at identifying the attitudes, stereotypes, and other hidden biases that affect people's perceptions, judgments, and actions.

The initiative has been widely covered in the media. But recently, researchers with the project have admitted it is not perfect. For the best results, project directors encourage individuals to take the test multiple times. The researchers say there is more value in aggregated results than in any individual test.

Los Angeles Clippers fans urged the NBA to force Donald Sterling to sell the team after the release of recordings of Sterling making racist comments.

fired after he tweeted that he was "uncomfortable" seeing a Japanese driver win the Indianapolis 500 auto race.[1]

SPORTS MEDIA AS CHANGE AGENTS

Just as a more diverse base of journalists reduced racial bias in earlier studies, diversity in the journalism ranks can also help call attention to the issue. Social media is making it easier for black sports journalists to create a platform for increased awareness of bias, both unconscious and deliberate. The development has not been without challenges, however.

In 2017, ESPN journalist Jemele Hill, a black woman, spoke out on Twitter about racism in the Trump presidential administration. Despite ESPN's policy encouraging its reporters to express themselves on social media, the network publicly reprimanded Hill. The reprimand led to an escalation of the issue, and ultimately, a request from the White House that Hill be fired. ESPN ignored the president's wishes, and the request itself generated discussion about the First Amendment threats created by an administration seeking to silence a journalist.

Hill's experience calls attention to another dimension of racism in sports and sports media. She was not the first journalist to criticize the presidential administration for racial bias. A white male editor of the *New Yorker* had published an even more critical assessment of the racist nature of the administration around that same time. Yet there was no such request for termination of that editor.

"Whenever black athletes [move] outside the box of going beyond just being the entertainment of society, it is met with tremendous blowback," said Hill. "It's all good when you're catching touchdown passes or when you score 30 points a game. But the moment you start talking about some issues of substance . . . it becomes a different situation."[2]

NO PLACE IN MEDIA FOR RACISM

In April 2017, the National Association of Broadcasters and the National Association of Broadcasters Education Foundation announced a new initiative to address racism in the media. The Awareness in Reporting tool kit is a collection of resources to help professional

NONRACIAL BIAS: PARA-ATHLETES STRUGGLE FOR EQUAL COVERAGE

Athletes of color are not the only group receiving a less-than-fair shot when it comes to attention both from sports fans and sports media. Para-athletes are also beginning to speak up about discrimination. In 2018, NBC stepped up to provide an unprecedented 94 hours of television coverage of the Winter Paralympic Games, which followed the PyeongChang Winter Olympics.[3] Advocates for para-athletes have been pleased that their competitions are receiving increased attention; however, their concerns mirror those of other groups who have battled discrimination. Many stories of para-athletes still focus on how they overcame their disabilities as opposed to their accomplishments and goals.

journalists improve their skills in covering race and racially sensitive news.

The tool kit offers a number of suggestions for reporters and editors. For example, one suggests that reporters make sure the race of the people they are reporting on is relevant to the story. For example, in a story about an argument between a white person and black person, there would be no reason to note their races unless the two were arguing about a racial issue.

Another suggestion pertains to word use and the negative mental pictures that some words create. Words such as "disadvantaged," "high-risk," and "inner city" can be viewed very negatively in particular communities.[6] Finally, the tool kit encourages reporters to expand their sources to include voices from all communities involved in the news event.

As the sports world becomes increasingly diverse, so too have the faces of the people covering the action on the sidelines and in press boxes from coast to coast. Pioneering journalists at all-black newspapers blazed a trail for today's writers and broadcasters. Meanwhile, white journalists have been challenged to examine their own biases as they report on athletes of color. It hasn't always been a smooth journey, and there's still more work to do. But the stories of people of color in the sports world today are being told in ways that are more representative of their experiences than ever before.

DISCUSSION STARTERS

- Are black sports journalists and white sports journalists being held to different standards when it comes to speaking out on racial issues? Discuss examples that support your case.

- Is firing sports journalists for racist and other inappropriate comments a good strategy to effect change? Why or why not?

ESSENTIAL FACTS

SIGNIFICANT EVENTS

- In 1908, Jack Johnson beats Tommy Burns to become the first black heavyweight boxing champion, forcing a segregated United States to acknowledge black success.

- Wendell Smith becomes the first black sportswriter to serve on the staff of a white newspaper (*Chicago Herald-American*) in 1948 after helping Jackie Robinson secure his groundbreaking spot on the Brooklyn Dodgers.

- Cassius Clay defeats Sonny Liston in 1964 for the world heavyweight title and announces he is converting to Islam and changing his name to Muhammad Ali, launching a career marked by a never-before-seen blend of athletic achievement, celebrity, and black activism.

- After analyzing NFL broadcasts, researchers Raymond Rainville and Edward McCormick conclude in 1977 that white players are more likely to be praised for good plays than black players, and black players are more likely to be criticized for bad plays than white players.

KEY PLAYERS

- Wendell Smith is a pioneer in the black press and also plays an important role in pushing the NFL and MLB to integrate.

- Sam Lacy writes for the *Washington Tribune* and the *Defender* and goes on to become the first black member of the Baseball Writers Association of America.

- Kenny Washington, a former UCLA football star, re-integrates the NFL with the Los Angeles Rams in 1946.

- Muhammad Ali challenges the white-dominated sports media to examine racial biases in its coverage of the outspoken heavyweight boxing champion.

- Howard Cosell, an influential white broadcaster, is one of Ali's most prominent allies in the sports media.

- LeBron James and other NBA players fight back against controversial policies and attacks from media outlets.

IMPACT ON SOCIETY

Sports reporting plays an important role in how people experience their culture. Problems arise when parts of a culture are either missing or are presented in an incomplete or inaccurate way. Robust representation of minority cultures in sports is particularly important, as those representations may be the primary way that people outside a culture experience it.

GLOSSARY

bias

Prejudice in favor of or against one thing, person, or group compared with another, usually in a way considered to be unfair.

boycott

A refusal to have dealings with another group, usually in order to express disapproval or to force acceptance of certain conditions.

brawn

Muscular strength.

foil

A person whose basic qualities contrast with those of a story's hero.

framing

Fitting or adjusting how a thing is perceived, especially for an end.

heavyweight

A fighter in the heaviest class of boxers.

Industrial Revolution

The rapid development of industry that occurred in Britain in the late 1700s and 1800s and migrated to the United States, brought about by the introduction of machinery.

Jim Crow laws

State and local laws passed in the 1880s in the South to racially segregate black people.

pardon

To cancel the consequences of a legal offense.

priming

Making someone ready to

segregation

The practice of separating groups of people based on race, gender, ethnicity, or other factors.

stereotype

ADDITIONAL RESOURCES

SELECTED BIBLIOGRAPHY

Lamb, Chris. *From Jack Johnson to LeBron James: Sports, Media, and the Color Line*. U of Nebraska P, 2016.

Runstedtler, Theresa. *Jack Johnson, Rebel Sojourner: Boxing in the Shadow of the Global Color Line*. U of California P, 2012.

Shropshire, Kenneth. *In Black and White: Race and Sports in America*. New York UP, 1996.

FURTHER READINGS

Abdul-Jabbar, Kareem. *Becoming Kareem: Growing Up On and Off the Court*. Little, Brown, 2017.

Maraniss, Andrew. *Strong Inside: The True Story of How Perry Wallace Broke College Basketball's Color Line*. Philomel, 2017.

Mirlis, Eric. *I Was There!: Joe Buck, Bob Costas, Jim Nantz, and Others Relive the Most Exciting Sporting Events of Their Lives*. Skyhorse, 2016.

ONLINE RESOURCES

Booklinks
NONFICTION NETWORK
FREE! ONLINE NONFICTION RESOURCES

To learn more about race in sports media coverage, visit abdobooklinks.com. These links are routinely monitored and updated to provide the most current information available.

MORE INFORMATION

For more information on this subject, contact or visit the following organizations:

THE INSTITUTE FOR DIVERSITY AND ETHICS IN SPORT
University of Central Florida
College of Business
4000 Central Florida Blvd.
Orlando, FL 32816
407-823-4887
tidesport.org

The institute researches and publishes studies that cover issues from across the spectrum of race and sports.

UNIVERSITY OF WISCONSIN PREJUDICE AND INTERGROUP RELATIONS LAB
Department of Psychology
Brodgen Hall
1202 West Johnson St.
Madison, WI 53706-1611
608-262-1040
sites.google.com/site/devinesocialpsych/

The lab researches how people manage the intrapersonal and interpersonal challenges associated with prejudice and stereotyping in contemporary society.

SOURCE NOTES

CHAPTER 1. JACK JOHNSON VS. JIM CROW

1. Theresa Runstedtler. *Jack Johnson, Rebel Sojourner: Boxing in the Shadow of the Global Color Line.* U of California P, 2012. 58–59.

2. Chris Lamb. *From Jack Johnson to LeBron James: Sports, Media, and the Color Line.* U of Nebraska P, 2016. 7–8.

3. Lamb, *From Jack Johnson to LeBron James*, 8–9.

4. "Shadow Boxing: The Journey of the African-American Fighter." *Sweet Science*, 1999. youtube.com. Accessed 12 Sept. 2018.

5. John Ridley. "A True Champion vs. The 'Great White Hope.'" *NPR*, 2 July 2010. npr.org. Accessed 12 Sept. 2018.

6. Lamb, *From Jack Johnson to LeBron James*, 9.

CHAPTER 2. SPORTS JOURNALISM AND THE BLACK PRESS

1. Brian Peter Moritz. "Rooting for the Story: Institutional Sports Journalism in the Digital Age." Dissertation, Syracuse University, 2014. 16.

CHAPTER 3. CONTRASTS IN COVERAGE

1. Chris Lamb. *From Jack Johnson to LeBron James: Sports, Media, and the Color Line.* U of Nebraska P, 2016. 58.

2. Ron Grossman. "Tidye Pickett: Chicago Track Star Was First African-American Female Olympian." *Chicago Tribune*, 19 Aug. 2016. chicagotribune.com. Accessed 12 Sept. 2018.

3. Emily Bonzagni. "Politics of Exclusion: An Analysis of the Intersections of Marginalized Identities and the Olympic Industry." Honors capstone project, Syracuse University, 2017. 26.

4. Lamb, *From Jack Johnson to LeBron James*, 105.

5. Nigel Collins. "Louis-Schmeling: More Than a Fight." *ESPN*, 19 June 2013. espn.com. Accessed 12 Sept. 2018.

6. Monte D. Cox. "Joe Louis, The Brown Bomber . . . 'His Punches Could Paralyze You.'" *Cox's Corner*, n.d., coxscorner.tripod.com. Accessed 12 Sept.

7. Lamb, *From Jack Johnson to LeBron James*, 8–9.

CHAPTER 4. BREAKING THE COLOR BARRIER

1. "Wendell Smith and Jackie Robinson." *Baseball Hall of Fame*, n.d., baseballhall.org. Accessed 12 Sept. 2018.

2. Chris Lamb. *From Jack Johnson to LeBron James: Sports, Media, and the Color Line.* U of Nebraska P, 2016. 109.

3. Nevada Cooke. "I Am America: The Chicago Defender on Joe Louis, Muhammad Ali, and Civil Rights, 1934–1975." MA thesis, University of Western Ontario, 2014. 104.

4. Kurt Badenhausen. "Michael Jordan Leads the NBA's Biggest Shoe Deals at $110 Million This Year." *Forbes*, 9 June 2017. forbes.com. Accessed 12 Sept. 2018.

5. Stephen A. Crockett Jr. "Michael Jordan: A Day Late and a Million Dollars Short." *Root*, 26 July 2016. theroot.com. Accessed 12 Sept. 2018.

6. Crockett Jr., "Michael Jordan."

7. Zachary Humphries. "Racial Bias in Professional Sports: From a Media and Fan Perspective." MA thesis, Youngstown State University, 2014. 6.

8. "The Black Athlete: An Editorial." *Sports Illustrated*. 5 Aug. 1968. si.com. Accessed 12 Sept. 2018.

CHAPTER 5. BLACK BRAWN AND WHITE BRAIN

1. Chris Lamb. *From Jack Johnson to LeBron James: Sports, Media, and the Color Line.* U of Nebraska P, 2016. 52.

2. "Ex-Redskin Alvin Garrett Recalls Remarkable Cosell." *Washington Post*, 25 Apr. 1995. washingtonpost.com. Accessed 12 Sept. 2018.

3. "Race and Sport." *Clark Science Center*, n.d. science.smith.edu. Accessed 15 Apr. 2018.

4. Susan Tyler Eastman and Andrew C. Billings. "Biased Voices of Sports: Racial and Gender Stereotyping in College Basketball Announcing." *Howard Journal of Communication*, vol. 12, no. 4, 2001. 190.

5. Noel Murray. "The Epic Celtics-Lakers Rivalry Inspires One of the Best *30 for 30s*." *A.V. Club*, 13 June 2017. tv.avclub.com. Accessed 12 Sept. 2018.

CHAPTER 6. A TALE OF TWO ATHLETES

1. Nathan Hurst. "Black Athletes Stereotyped Negatively in Media Compared to White Athletes." *University of Missouri News Bureau*, 2 June 2015. munews.missouri.edu. Accessed 12 Sept. 2018.

2. Jill Martin. "Study: NFL Arrest Rate Lower Than for All Males Age 20 to 39." *CNN*, 26 Aug. 2015. cnn.com. Accessed 12 Sept. 2018.

3. Edward Schumacher-Matos. "Ethics, Morality and a Ticking Clock for How to Report on the R**skins." *NPR*, 19 Mar. 2014. npr.org. Accessed 12 Sept. 2018.

CHAPTER 7. SOCIAL MEDIA: THE NEW HEAVYWEIGHT

1. Jasneel Chaddha. "The New Face of Sports Media." *Huffington Post*, 29 Aug. 2017. huffingtonpost.com. Accessed 12 Sept. 2018.

2. Chaddha, "The New Face of Sports Media."

3. "Selected Global Media and Sporting Events with the Most Facebook Interactions as of May 2017." *Statista*, n.d. statista.com. Accessed 12 Sept. 2018.

4. Ian Cary. "What's with All the Racist Tweets, Sports Fans?" *Huffington Post*, 27 Apr. 2012. huffingtonpost.com. Accessed 12 Sept. 2018.

5. Emily Sullivan. "Laura Ingraham Told LeBron James to Shut Up and Dribble; He Went to the Hoop." *NPR*, 19 Feb. 2018. npr.org. Accessed 12 Sept. 2018.

CHAPTER 8. FRAMING RACISM IN SPORTS MEDIA

1. Gordon Cox. "Hollywood Diversity and Inclusion See Little Rise in 10 Years." *Variety*, 31 July 2017. variety.com. Accessed 12 Sept. 2018.

2. Cristina Marcos. "115th Congress Will Be Most Racially Diverse in History." *Hill*, 17 Nov. 2016. thehill.com. Accessed 12 Sept. 2018.

3. Grace Donnelly. "The Number of Black CEOs at Fortune 500 Companies Is at Its Lowest Since 2002." *Fortune*, 28 Feb. 2018. fortune.com. Accessed 12 Sept. 2018.

4. Richard E. Lapchick. "Crime and Athletes: New Racial Stereotypes." *Society*, vol. 37, no. 3, 2000. link.springer.com. Accessed 12 Sept. 2018.

5. "Iowa High School Basketball Broadcasters Fired for Racist Commentary." *WQAD News*, 4 Dec. 2017. wqad.com. Accessed 12 Sept. 2018.

CHAPTER 9. LEVELING THE PLAYING FIELD

1. Ruth Brown. "Reporter Gets Fired for Racist Indy 500 Tweet." *New York Post*, 29 May 2017. nypost.com. Accessed 12 Sept. 2018.

2. Gene Demby. "ESPN's Jemele Hill on Race, Football, and That Tweet about Trump." *NPR*, 4 Jan. 2018. npr.org. Accessed 12 Sept. 2018.

3. "NBC Olympics to Present Unprecedented 94 Hours of Paralympic Television Coverage in March." *US Olympic Committee*, 29 Jan. 2018. teamusa.org. Accessed 12 Sept. 2018.

4. Richard Lapchick et al. "The 2018 Associated Press Sports Editors Racial and Gender Report Card." *TIDES*, 2 May 2018. tidesport.org. Accessed 12 Sept. 2018.

5. Lapchick et al. "The 2018 Associated Press Sports Editors Racial and Gender Report Card."

6. "Reporters, Producers and Writers." *Awareness in Reporting*, n.d. awarenessinreporting.org. Accessed 12 Sept. 2018.

INDEX

DUCHESS HARRIS, JD, PHD

Professor Harris is the chair of the American Studies department at Macalester College and curator of the Duchess Harris Collection of ABDO books. She is the author and coauthor of recently released ABDO books including *Hidden Human Computers: The Black Women of NASA*, *Black Lives Matter*, and *Race and Policing*.

Before working with ABDO, she authored several other books on the topics of race, culture, and American history. She served as an associate editor for *Litigation News*, the American Bar Association Section of Litigation's quarterly flagship publication, and was the first editor in chief of *Law Raza*, an interactive online journal covering race and the law, published at William Mitchell College of Law. She has earned a PhD in American Studies from the University of Minnesota and a JD from William Mitchell College of Law.

JILL C. WHEELER

Jill C. Wheeler is the author of more than 300 nonfiction titles for young readers. Her interests include biographies along with the natural and behavioral sciences. She lives in Minneapolis, Minnesota, where she enjoys sailing, riding motorcycles, and reading.